D0636484

ESSENTIAL
Chocolate

Contents

Introduction

Chocolate is one of life's luxuries and one of the few that we can all afford. This book contains all of the recipes you need to enjoy this luxury at any time of day. For example, you could wake up to pain au chocolate with morning coffee, indulge in a hot chocolate pudding at lunchtime, have a sumptuous slice of chocolate cake with afternoon tea, and round off the day with a hot chocolate drink.

Chocolate is produced from the beans of the cacao tree. These are found within large pods, which once harvested, both the pulp from the pods and the beans are fermented in the sun to develop the chocolatey flavour. The outer skin is then removed and the beans are left in the sun for a while longer or roasted. Finally, they are shelled and the kernels are used for making cocoa and chocolate.

Once ground and processed, the kernels produce 'cocoa solids', from this we gauge the quality of the chocolate. The cocoa solids are then pressed to remove some of the fat – 'cocoa butter'. They are then further processed to produce the product that we know and love as chocolate.

Chocolate is very versatile, therefore wonderful toppings and decoration such as chocolate caraque can be made from it. To make chocolate caraque spread melted chocolate on a marble or acrylic board. As it begins to set, pull a knife through the chocolate at 45°C angle, working quickly. Remove each caraque as you make it and chill firmly before using.

There are many different types of chocolate, each with its own distinctive taste and use. Dark Chocolate can contain anything from 30% to 75% cocoa solids. It has a slightly sweet flavour and a dark colour, and is mostly used in cooking. The majority of these recipes need around 50% cocoa solids.

Milk Chocolate contains milk and has a lovely creamy, sweet flavour. It is mostly used as an eating chocolate. White Chocolate contains a lower cocoa butter content and less cocoa solids than milk chocolate. It can be quite temperamental when used in cooking, so always choose a luxury white cooking chocolate.

Couverture retains a high gloss after melting and cooling; however, it requires tempering and is only available from specialist suppliers. Chocolate-Flavoured Cake Covering is an inferior product that has a higher fat content making it easier to handle when making some decorations.

Many recipes require chocolate chips; these are available in dark, milk and white chocolate varieties and are used for baking and decoration.

Cocoa Powder is the powder left after the cocoa butter has been pressed. It is unsweetened but gives a strong chocolate flavour when used in cooking.

Chocolate Tray Bake

Serves 15

INGREDIENTS

350 g/12 oz/3 cups self-raising
flour, sieved (strained)

3 tbsp cocoa powder, sieved
(strained)

225 g/8 oz/1 cup caster
(superfine) sugar

225 g/8 oz/1 cup soft margarine

4 eggs, beaten

4 tbsp milk

50 g/1³/₄ oz/¹/₃ cup milk
chocolate chips

50 g/1³/₄ oz/¹/₃ cup dark
chocolate chips

50 g/1³/₄ oz/¹/₃ cup white
chocolate chips

icing (confectioners') sugar,
to dust

1 Grease a 33 x 24 x 5 cm/
13 x 9 x 2 inch cake tin
(pan) with a little butter or
margarine.

2 Place all of the
ingredients except for
the chocolate chips and
icing (confectioners') sugar
in a large mixing bowl and
beat together until smooth.

3 Beat in the milk, dark
and white chocolate
chips.

4 Spoon the mixture into
the prepared cake tin
(pan) and level the top.

Bake in a preheated oven,
180°C/350°F/Gas Mark 4,
for 30-40 minutes until
risen and springy to the
touch. Leave to cool in the
tin (pan).

5 Once cool, dust with
icing (confectioners')
sugar. Cut into squares
to serve.

COOK'S TIP

*If liked, serve warm with
whipped cream for a
delicious dessert.*

COOK'S TIP

*The cake can be frozen,
wrapped well in the tin
(pan), for 2 months. Defrost
at room temperature.*

VARIATION

*For an attractive finish, cut
thin strips of paper and lay
in a criss-cross pattern on top
of the cake. Dust with icing
(confectioners') sugar, then
remove the paper strips.*

Chocolate & Orange Cake

Serves 8-10

INGREDIENTS

175 g/6 oz/³/₄ cup caster (superfine) sugar	flour, sieved (strained)	ICING:
	2 tbsp cocoa powder, sieved (strained)	175 g/6 oz/1 cup icing (confectioners') sugar
175 g/6 oz/³/₄ cup butter or block margarine	2 tbsp milk	2 tbsp orange juice
3 eggs, beaten	3 tbsp orange juice	
175 g/6 oz/1¹/₂ cups self-raising	grated rind of ¹/₂ orange	

1 Lightly grease a 20 cm/ 8 inch deep round cake tin (pan).

2 Beat together the sugar and butter or margarine in a bowl until light and fluffy. Gradually add the eggs, beating well after each addition. Carefully fold in the flour.

3 Divide the mixture in half. Add the cocoa powder and milk to one half, stirring until well combined. Flavour the other half with the orange juice and rind.

4 Place spoonfuls of each mixture into the prepared tin (pan) and swirl together with a skewer, to create a marbled effect. Bake in a preheated oven, 190°C/375°F/Gas Mark 5, for 25 minutes or until springy to the touch.

5 Leave the cake to cool in the tin (pan) for a few minutes before transferring to a wire rack to cool completely.

6 To make the icing, sift the icing (confectioners') sugar into a mixing bowl

and mix in enough of the orange juice to form a smooth icing. Spread the icing over the top of the cake and leave to set before serving.

VARIATION

Add 2 tablespoons of rum or brandy to the chocolate mixture instead of the milk. The cake also works well when flavoured with grated lemon rind and juice instead of the orange.

Mocha Layer Cake

Serves 8–10

200 g/7³/4 oz/1 cup self-raising
    flour
¹/4 tsp baking powder
4 tbsp cocoa powder
100 g/3¹/2 oz/7 tbsp caster
    (superfine) sugar
2 eggs
2 tbsp golden (light corn) syrup

150 ml/¹/4 pint/²/3 cup
    sunflower oil
150 ml/¹/4 pint/²/3 cup milk

FILLING:
1 tsp instant coffee
1 tbsp boiling water
300 ml/¹/2 pint/1¹/4 cups double
    (heavy) cream

25 g/1 oz/2 tbsp icing
    (confectioners') sugar

TO DECORATE:
50 g/1³/4 oz flock chocolate
chocolate caraque (see
    introduction)
icing (confectioners') sugar,
    to dust

1 Lightly grease three 18 cm/7 inch cake tins (pans).

2 Sieve (strain) the flour, baking powder and cocoa powder into a large mixing bowl. Stir in the sugar. Make a well in the centre and stir in the eggs, syrup, oil and milk. Beat with a wooden spoon, gradually mixing in the dry ingredients to make a smooth batter. Divide the mixture between the prepared tins (pans).

3 Bake in a preheated oven, 180°C/350°F/Gas Mark 4, for 35–45 minutes or until springy to the touch. Leave in the tins (pans) for 5 minutes, then turn out on to a wire rack to cool completely.

4 Dissolve the instant coffee in the boiling water and place in a bowl with the cream and icing (confectioners') sugar. Whip until the cream is just holding it's shape. Use half of the cream to sandwich the 3 cakes together. Spread the remaining cream over the top and sides of the cake. Lightly press the flock chocolate into the cream around the edge of the cake.

5 Transfer to a serving plate. Lay the caraque over the top of the cake. Cut a few thin strips of baking parchment and place on top of the caraque. Dust lightly with icing (confectioners') sugar, then carefully remove the paper. Serve.

Devil's Food Cake

Serves 8

INGREDIENTS

100 g/3¹/₂ oz dark chocolate
250 g/9 oz/2¹/₄ cups self-raising flour
1 tsp bicarbonate of soda (baking soda)
225 g/8 oz/1 cup butter

400 g/14 oz/2²/₃ cups dark muscovado sugar
1 tsp vanilla flavouring (extract)
3 eggs
125 ml/4 fl oz/¹/₂ cup buttermilk
225 ml/8 fl oz/2 cups boiling water

FROSTING:
300 g/10¹/₂ oz/1¹/₃ cups caster (superfine) sugar
2 egg whites
1 tbsp lemon juice
3 tbsp orange juice
candied orange peel, to decorate

1 Lightly grease two 20 cm/8 inch shallow round cake tins (pans) and line the bases. Melt the chocolate in a pan. Sieve (strain) the flour and bicarbonate of soda (baking soda) together.

2 Beat the butter and sugar in a bowl until pale and fluffy. Beat in the vanilla flavouring (extract) and the eggs, one at a time and beating well after each addition. Add a little flour if the mixture begins to curdle.

3 Fold the melted chocolate into the mixture until well blended. Gradually fold in the remaining flour, then stir in the buttermilk and boiling water.

4 Divide the mixture between the tins (pans) and level the tops. Bake in a preheated oven, 190°C/375°F/Gas Mark 5, for 30 minutes until springy to the touch. Leave to cool in the tin (pan) for 5 minutes, then transfer to a wire rack to cool completely.

5 Place the frosting ingredients in a large bowl set over a pan of gently simmering water. Whisk, preferably with an electric beater, until thickened and forming soft peaks. Remove from the heat and whisk until the mixture is cool.

6 Sandwich the 2 cakes together with a little of the frosting, then spread the remainder over the sides and top of the cake, swirling it as you do so. Decorate with the candied orange peel.

Chocolate Passion Cake

Serves 10–12

INGREDIENTS

5 eggs
150 g/5$^{1}/_{2}$ oz/$^{2}/_{3}$ cup caster (superfine) sugar
150 g/5$^{1}/_{2}$ oz/1$^{1}/_{4}$ cups plain (all-purpose) flour
40 g/1$^{1}/_{2}$ oz/$^{1}/_{3}$ cup cocoa powder

175 g/6 oz carrots, peeled and finely grated
50 g/1$^{3}/_{4}$ oz/$^{1}/_{2}$ cup chopped walnuts
2 tbsp sunflower oil
350 g/12 oz medium fat soft cheese

175 g/6 oz/1 cup icing (confectioners') sugar
175 g/6 oz milk or dark chocolate, melted

1 Lightly grease and line the base of a 20 cm/8 inch deep round cake tin (pan).

2 Place the eggs and sugar in a large mixing bowl set over a pan of gently simmering water and whisk until very thick. Lift the whisk up and let the mixture drizzle back – it will leave a trail for a few seconds when thick enough.

3 Remove the bowl from the heat. Sieve (strain) the flour and cocoa powder into the bowl and carefully fold in. Fold in the carrots, walnuts and oil until just combined.

4 Pour into the prepared tin (pan) and bake in a preheated oven, 190°C/375°F/Gas Mark 5, for 45 minutes or until well risen and springy to the touch. Leave to cool slightly then turn out on to a wire rack to cool completely.

5 Beat together the soft cheese and icing (confectioners') sugar until combined. Beat in the melted chocolate. Split the cake in half and sandwich together again with half of the chocolate mixture. Cover the top of the cake with the remainder of the chocolate mixture, swirling it with a knife. Leave to chill or serve at once.

COOK'S TIP

The undecorated cake can be frozen for up to 2 months. Defrost at room temperature for 3 hours or overnight in the refrigerator.

Sachertorte

Serves 10–12

INGREDIENTS

175 g/6 oz dark chocolate
150 g/5$\frac{1}{2}$ oz/$\frac{2}{3}$ cup unsalted butter
150 g/5$\frac{1}{2}$ oz/$\frac{2}{3}$ cup caster (superfine) sugar
6 eggs, separated

150 g/5$\frac{1}{2}$ oz/1$\frac{1}{4}$ cups plain (all-purpose) flour

ICING AND FILLING:
175 g/6 oz dark chocolate
5 tbsp strong black coffee

175 g/6 oz/1 cup icing (confectioners') sugar
6 tbsp good apricot preserve
50 g/1$\frac{3}{4}$ oz dark chocolate, melted

1 Grease a 23 cm/9 inch springform cake tin (pan) and line the base. Melt the chocolate. Beat the butter and 75 g/2$\frac{3}{4}$ oz/$\frac{1}{3}$ cup of the sugar until pale and fluffy. Add the egg yolks and beat well. Add the chocolate in a thin stream, beating well. Sieve (strain) the flour; fold it into the mixture. Whisk the egg whites until they stand in soft peaks. Add the remaining sugar and whisk for 2 minutes by hand, or 45–60 seconds if using an electric whisk, until glossy. Fold half into the chocolate mixture, then fold in the remainder.

2 Spoon into the prepared tin (pan) and level the top. Bake in a preheated oven, 150°C/300°F/ Gas Mark 2, for 1–1$\frac{1}{4}$ hours until a skewer inserted into the centre comes out clean. Cool in the tin (pan) for 5 minutes, then transfer to a wire rack to cool completely.

3 To make the icing, melt the chocolate and beat in the coffee until smooth. Sieve (strain) the icing (confectioners') sugar into a bowl. Whisk in the melted chocolate mixture to give a thick icing. Halve the cake.

Warm the jam, spread over one half of the cake and sandwich together. Invert the cake on a wire rack. Spoon the icing over the cake and spread to coat the top and sides. Leave to set for 5 minutes, allowing any excess icing to drop through the rack. Transfer to a serving plate and leave to set for at least 2 hours.

4 To decorate, spoon the melted chocolate into a small piping bag and pipe the word 'Sacher' or 'Sachertorte' on the top of the cake. Leave it to harden before serving the cake.

Dark & White Chocolate Torte

Serves 10

INGREDIENTS

4 eggs
100 g/3¹/₂ oz/7 tbsp cup caster
(superfine) sugar
100 g/3¹/₂ oz/³/₄ cup plain (all-
purpose) flour

DARK CHOCOLATE CREAM:
300 ml/¹/₂ pint/²/₃ cup double
(heavy) cream
150 g/5¹/₂ oz dark chocolate,
broken into small pieces

WHITE CHOCOLATE ICING:
75 g/2³/₄ oz white chocolate
15 g/¹/₂ oz/1 tbsp butter
1 tbsp milk
50 g/1³/₄ oz/4 tbsp icing
(confectioners') sugar
chocolate caraque (see introduction)

1 Grease a 20 cm/8 inch round springform tin (pan) and line the base. Whisk the eggs and caster (superfine) sugar in a large mixing bowl with electric beaters for about 10 minutes, or until the mixture is very light and foamy and the whisk leaves a trail that lasts a few seconds when lifted.

2 Sieve (strain) the flour and fold in with a metal spoon or spatula. Pour into the prepared tin (pan) and bake in a preheated oven, 180°C/350°F/Gas Mark 4,

for 35–40 minutes, or until springy to the touch. Leave to cool slightly, then transfer to a wire rack to cool completely. Cut the cold cake into 2 layers.

3 To make the chocolate cream, place the cream in a saucepan and bring to the boil, stirring. Add the chocolate and stir until melted and well combined. Remove from the heat and leave to cool. Beat with a wooden spoon until thick.

4 Sandwich the 2 cake layers back together

with the chocolate cream and place on a wire rack.

5 To make the icing, melt the chocolate and butter together and stir until blended. Whisk in the milk and icing (confectioners') sugar. Whisk for a few minutes until the icing is cool. Pour it over the cake and spread with a palette knife (spatula) to coat the top and sides. Decorate with chocolate caraque and leave to set.

Bûche de Noël

Serves 8–10

INGREDIENTS

CAKE:

4 eggs

100 g/3¹/² oz/7 tbsp caster
    (superfine) sugar

75 g/2³/⁴ oz/²/³ cup self-raising
    flour

2 tbsp cocoa powder

ICING:

150 g/5¹/² oz dark chocolate

2 egg yolks

150 ml/¹/⁴ pint/²/³ cup milk

125 g/4¹/² oz/¹/² cup butter

50 g/1³/⁴ oz/4 tbsp icing
    (confectioners') sugar

2 tbsp rum (optional)

TO DECORATE:

a little white glacé or royal icing

icing (confectioners') sugar, to
    dust

holly or Christmas cake
    decorations

1 Grease and line a 30 x 23 cm/12 x 9 inch Swiss roll tin (pan). Whisk the eggs and caster (superfine) sugar in a bowl with electric beaters for 10 minutes, or until the mixture is very light and foamy and the whisk leaves a trail. Sieve (strain) the flour and cocoa powder and fold in. Pour into the prepared tin (pan) and bake in a preheated oven, 200°C/400°F/Gas Mark 6, for 12 minutes or until springy to the touch. Turn out on to a piece of baking parchment which

has been sprinkled with a little caster (superfine) sugar. Peel off the lining paper and trim the edges. Cut a small slit halfway into the cake about 1 cm/½ inch from one short end. Starting at that end, roll up tightly, enclosing the paper. Place on a wire rack to cool.

2 To make the icing, break the chocolate into pieces and melt it over a pan of hot water. Beat in the egg yolks, whisk in the milk and cook until the mixture thickens enough to coat the

back of a wooden spoon, stirring. Cover with dampened greaseproof paper and cool. Beat the butter and sugar until pale and fluffy. Beat in the custard and rum, if using. Unroll the sponge, spread with one-third of the icing and roll up again. Place on a serving plate. Spread the remaining icing over the cake and mark with a fork to give the effect of bark. Leave to set. Pipe white icing to form the rings of the log. Sprinkle with sugar and decorate.

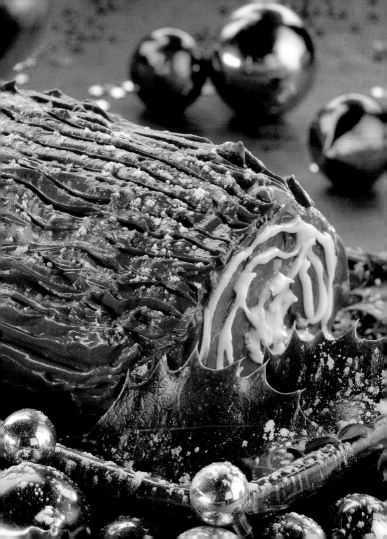

White Chocolate Truffle Cake

Serves 12

INGREDIENTS

2 eggs

50 g/1³/4 oz/4 tbsp caster (superfine) sugar

50 g/1³/4 oz/¹/3 cup plain (all-purpose) flour

50 g/1³/4 oz white chocolate,

melted

TRUFFLE TOPPING:

300 ml/¹/2 pint/1¹/4 cups double (heavy) cream

350 g/12 oz white chocolate, broken into pieces

250 g/9 oz Quark or fromage frais

TO DECORATE:

dark, milk or white chocolate, melted

cocoa powder, to dust

1 Grease a 20 cm/8 inch round springform tin (pan) and line the base. Whisk the eggs and caster (superfine) sugar in a mixing bowl for 10 minutes, or until the mixture is very light and foamy and the whisk leaves a trail that lasts a few seconds when lifted. Sieve (strain) the flour and fold in with a metal spoon. Fold in the melted white chocolate. Pour into the tin (pan) and bake in a preheated oven, 180°C/350°F/Gas Mark 4, for 25 minutes or until springy to the touch. Leave to cool

slightly, then transfer to a wire rack until completely cold. Return the cold cake to the tin (pan).

2 To make the topping, place the cream in a pan and bring to the boil, stirring to prevent it sticking to the bottom of the pan. Cool slightly, then add the white chocolate pieces and stir until melted and combined. Remove from the heat and leave until almost cool, stirring, then stir in the Quark or fromage frais. Pour the mixture on top of the cake and chill for

2 hours. Remove the cake from the tin (pan) and transfer to a serving plate.

3 To make large chocolate curls, pour melted chocolate on to a marble or acrylic board and spread it thinly with a palette knife (spatula). Leave to set at room temperature. Using a scraper, push through the chocolate at a 25° angle until a large curl forms. Remove each curl as you make it and leave to chill until set. Decorate the cake with chocolate curls and sprinkle with a little cocoa powder.

Tropical Fruit Vacherin

Serves 10–12

INGREDIENTS

6 egg whites
275 g/9^{1}/2 oz/generous 1 cup caster (superfine) sugar
75 g/2^{3}/4 oz/^{3}/4 cup desiccated (shredded) coconut

FILLING AND TOPPING:
90 g/3 oz dark chocolate, broken into pieces
3 egg yolks
3 tbsp water
1 tbsp rum (optional)

50 g/1^{3}/4 oz/4 tbsp caster (superfine) sugar
450 ml/16 fl oz/2 cups double (heavy) cream
selection of tropical fruits, sliced or cut into bite size pieces

1 Draw 3 circles, 20 cm/ 8 inch each, on sheets of baking parchment and place on baking trays (cookie sheets).

2 Whisk the egg whites until standing in soft peaks, then gradually whisk in half of the sugar and continue whisking until the mixture is very stiff and glossy. Carefully fold in the remaining sugar and the coconut.

3 Spoon the mixture into a piping bag fitted with a star nozzle (tip) and cover the circles with piped swirls. Bake in a preheated oven, 140°C/275°F/Gas Mark 1, for 1½ hours, changing the position of the trays (sheets) halfway through. Without opening the oven door, turn off the oven and leave the meringues to cool in the oven, then peel away the paper.

4 To make the filling, place the chocolate pieces, egg yolks, water, rum, if using, and sugar in a small bowl and place it over a pan of gently simmering water.

Cook over a low heat, stirring, until the chocolate has melted and the mixture has thickened. Cover with a disc of baking parchment and leave until cold.

5 Whip the cream and fold two-thirds of it into the chocolate mixture. Sandwich the meringue layers together with the chocolate mixture. Place the remaining cream in a piping bag fitted with a star nozzle (tip) and pipe around the edge of the meringue. Arrange the tropical fruits in the centre.

Chocolate Dairy Wraps

Makes 6–8

INGREDIENTS

2 eggs 50 g/1³/4 oz/4 tbsp caster (superfine) sugar	50 g/1³/4 oz/¹/3 cup plain (all-purpose) flour 1¹/2 tbsp cocoa powder 4 tbsp apricot jam	150 ml/¹/4 pint/²/3 cup double (heavy) cream, whipped icing (confectioners') sugar, to dust

1 Line 2 baking trays (cookie sheets) with pieces of baking parchment. Whisk the eggs and sugar together until the mixture is very light and fluffy and the whisk leaves a trail when lifted.

2 Sift together the flour and cocoa powder. Using a metal spoon or a spatula, gently fold it into the eggs and sugar in a figure of eight movement.

3 Drop rounded tablespoons of the mixture on to the lined baking trays (cookie sheets) and spread them into oval shapes. Make sure they are well spaced as they will spread during cooking.

4 Bake in a preheated oven, 220°C/425°F/Gas Mark 7, for about 6–8 minutes or until springy to the touch. Leave to cool on the baking trays (cookie sheets).

5 When cold, slide the cakes on to a damp tea towel and allow to stand until cold. Carefully remove them from the dampened paper. Spread the flat side of the cakes with jam, then spoon or pipe the whipped cream down the centre of each one.

6 Fold the cakes in half and place them on a serving plate. Sprinkle them with a little icing (confectioners') sugar and serve.

VARIATION

Fold 4 tsp of crème de menthe or 50 g/2 oz melted chocolate into the cream for fabulous alternatives to plain dairy cream.

Chocolate Cup Cakes with White Chocolate Icing

Makes 18

INGREDIENTS

100 g/3 1/2 oz/ generous 1/3 cup
   butter, softened
100 g/3 1/2 oz/7 tbsp caster
   (superfine) sugar
2 eggs, lightly beaten

50 g/1 3/4 oz/1/3 cup dark
   chocolate chips
2 tbsp milk
150 g/5 1/2 oz/1 1/4 cups self-
   raising flour
25 g/1 oz/1/4 cup cocoa powder

ICING:
225 g/8 oz white chocolate
150 g/5 1/2 oz low-fat soft cheese

1 Line an 18 hole bun tray with individual paper cup cases.

2 Beat together the butter and sugar until pale and fluffy. Gradually add the eggs, beating well after each addition. Add a little of the flour if the mixture begins to curdle. Add the milk, then fold in the chocolate chips.

3 Sift together the flour and cocoa powder and fold into the mixture with a metal spoon or spatula. Divide the mixture equally between the paper cases and level the tops.

4 Bake in a preheated oven, 180°C/350°F/Gas Mark 4, for 20 minutes, or until well risen and springy to the touch. Leave to cool on a wire rack.

5 To make the icing, melt the chocolate, then leave to cool slightly. Beat the cream cheese until softened slightly, then beat in the melted chocolate. Spread a little of the icing over each cake and chill for 1 hour before serving.

VARIATION

Add white chocolate chips or chopped pecan nuts to the mixture instead of the dark chocolate chips, if you prefer. You can also add the finely grated rind of 1 orange for a chocolate and orange flavour.

Chocolate Rum Babas

Makes 4

INGREDIENTS

100 g/3¹/2 oz/³/4 cup strong plain (all-purpose) flour
25 g/1 oz/¹/4 cup cocoa powder
6 g sachet easy blend yeast
pinch of salt
15 g/¹/2 oz/1 tbsp caster (superfine) sugar

40 g/1¹/2 oz dark chocolate, grated
2 eggs
3 tbsp tepid milk
50 g/1³/4 oz/4 tbsp butter, melted

SYRUP:
4 tbsp clear honey

2 tbsp water
4 tbsp rum

TO SERVE:
whipped cream
cocoa powder, to dust
fresh fruit (optional)

---

1 Lightly oil 4 individual ring tins (pans). In a large warmed mixing bowl, sieve (strain) the flour and cocoa powder together. Stir in the yeast, salt, sugar and grated chocolate. Beat the eggs together, add the milk and butter and beat until mixed.

2 Make a well in the centre of the dry ingredients and pour in the egg mixture, beating to mix to a batter. Beat for 10 minutes, ideally in a electric mixer with a dough hook.

Divide the mixture between the tins (pans) – it should come halfway up the sides.

3 Place on a baking tray (cookie sheet) and cover with a damp tea towel. Leave in a warm place until the mixture rises almost to the tops of the tins (pans). Bake in a preheated oven, 200°C/ 400°F/ Gas Mark 6, for 15 minutes.

4 To make the syrup, gently heat all of the ingredients in a small pan.

Turn out the babas and place on rack placed above a tray to catch the syrup. Drizzle the syrup over the babas and leave for at least 2 hours for the syrup to soak in. Once or twice, spoon the syrup that has dripped on to the tray over the babas.

5 Fill the centre of the babas with whipped cream and sprinkle a little cocoa powder over the top. Serve the babas with fresh fruit, if desired.

Chocolate Fudge Brownies

Makes 16

INGREDIENTS

200 g/7 oz low-fat soft cheese
$\frac{1}{2}$ tsp vanilla flavouring (extract)
2 eggs
250 g/9 oz/generous 1 cup caster
   (superfine) sugar

100 g/3$\frac{1}{2}$ oz/generous $\frac{1}{3}$ cup
   butter
3 tbsp cocoa powder
100 g/3$\frac{1}{2}$ oz/$\frac{3}{4}$ cup self-raising
   flour, sieved (strained)
50 g/1$\frac{3}{4}$ oz pecans, chopped

FUDGE ICING:
50 g/1$\frac{3}{4}$ oz/1 tbsp butter
1 tbsp milk
100 g/3$\frac{1}{2}$ oz/$\frac{1}{2}$ cup icing
   (confectioners') sugar
2 tbsp cocoa powder
pecans, to decorate (optional)

1 Lightly grease a 20 cm/8 inch square shallow cake tin (pan) and line the base.

2 Beat together the cheese, vanilla flavouring (extract) and 25 g/1 oz/5 tsp of the caster (superfine) sugar until smooth, then set aside.

3 Beat the eggs and remaining caster (superfine) sugar together until light and fluffy. Place the butter and cocoa powder in a small pan and heat gently, stirring until the butter melts and the mixture combines, then stir it into the egg mixture. Fold in the flour and nuts.

4 Pour half of the brownie mixture into the tin (pan) and level the top. Carefully spread the soft cheese over it, then cover it with the remaining brownie mixture. Bake in a preheated oven, 180°C/350°F/Gas Mark 4, for 40–45 minutes. Cool in the tin (pan).

5 To make the icing, melt the butter in the milk. Stir in the icing (confectioners') sugar and cocoa powder. Spread the icing over the brownies and decorate with pecan nuts, if using. Leave the icing to set, then cut into squares to serve.

VARIATION

Omit the cheese layer if preferred. Use walnuts in place of the pecans.

Chocolate Chip Muffins

Makes 12

INGREDIENTS

100 g/3¹/2 oz/generous ¹/3 cup
    soft margarine
225 g/8 oz/1 cup caster
    (superfine) sugar
2 large eggs

150 ml/¹/4 pint/²/3 cup whole
    milk natural yogurt
5 tbsp milk
275 g/9¹/2 oz/2 cups plain
    (all-purpose) flour

1 tsp bicarbonate of soda
    (baking soda)
175 g/6 oz dark chocolate chips

1 Line 12 muffin tins (pans) with paper cases.

2 Place the margarine and sugar in a large mixing bowl and beat with a wooden spoon until light and fluffy. Beat in the eggs, yogurt and milk until combined.

3 Sieve (strain) the flour and bicarbonate of soda (baking soda) together and add to the mixture. Stir until just blended.

4 Stir in the chocolate chips, then spoon the mixture into the paper cases and bake in a preheated oven, 190°C/375°F/Gas Mark 5, for 25 minutes or until a fine skewer inserted into the centre comes out clean. Leave to cool in the tin (pan) for 5 minutes, then turn out on to a wire rack to cool completely.

VARIATION

For chocolate and orange muffins, add the grated rind of 1 orange and replace the milk with fresh orange juice.

VARIATION

The mixture can also be used to make 6 large or 24 mini muffins. Bake mini muffins for 10 minutes or until springy to the touch.

Pain au Chocolate

Makes 12

INGREDIENTS

450 g/1 lb/4 cups strong plain (all-purpose) flour
1/2 tsp salt
6 g sachet of easy blend yeast
25 g/1 oz/2 tbsp white vegetable fat

1 egg, beaten lightly
225 ml/8 fl oz/1 cup tepid water
175 g/6 oz/3/4 cup butter, softened

100 g/31/2 oz dark chocolate, broken into 12 squares
beaten egg, to glaze
icing (confectioners') sugar, to dust

1 Lightly grease a baking tray (cookie sheet). Sieve (strain) the flour and salt into a mixing bowl and stir in the yeast. Rub in the fat with your fingertips. Add the egg and enough of the water to mix to a soft dough. Knead it for about 10 minutes to make a smooth elastic dough.

2 Roll out to form a rectangle 37.5 x 20 cm/ 15 x 8 inches. Divide the butter into 3 portions and dot one portion over two-thirds of the rectangle, leaving a small border around the edge.

3 Fold the rectangle into 3 by first folding the plain part of the dough over and then the other side. Seal the edges of the dough by pressing with a rolling pin. Give the dough a quarter turn so the sealed edges are at the top and bottom. Re-roll and fold (without adding butter), then wrap the dough and chill for 30 minutes.

4 Repeat steps 2 and 3 until all of the butter has been used, chilling the dough each time. Re-roll and fold twice more without butter. Chill for a final 30 minutes.

5 Roll the dough to a rectangle 45 x 30 cm/18 x 12 inches, trim and halve lengthways. Cut each half into 6 rectangles and brush with beaten egg. Place a chocolate square at one end of each rectangle and roll up to form a sausage. Press the ends together and place, seamside down, on the baking tray (cookie sheet). Cover and leave to rise for 40 minutes in a warm place. Brush with egg and bake in a preheated oven, 220°C/425°F/Gas Mark 7, for 20–25 minutes until golden. Cool on a wire rack. Serve warm or cold.

Chocolate & Coconut Squares

Makes 9

INGREDIENTS

225 g/8 oz dark chocolate digestive biscuits (graham crackers)	1 egg, beaten	flour, sieved (strained)
75 g/2³/4 oz/¹/3 cup butter or margarine	1 tsp vanilla flavouring (extract)	125 g/4¹/2 oz/1¹/3 cups desiccated (shredded) coconut
170 g/6 oz can evaporated milk	25 g/1 oz/5 tsp caster (superfine) sugar	50 g/1³/4 oz dark chocolate (optional)
	50 g/1³/4 oz/¹/3 cup self-raising	

1 Grease a shallow 20 cm/ 8 inch square cake tin (pan) and line the base.

2 Crush the biscuits (crackers) in a polythene bag with a rolling pin or process them in a food processor.

3 Melt the butter or margarine in a saucepan and stir in the crushed biscuits (crackers) until well combined.

4 Press the mixture into the base of the cake tin (pan).

5 Beat together the evaporated milk, egg, vanilla and sugar until smooth. Stir in the flour and desiccated (shredded) coconut. Pour over the biscuit base and level the top.

6 Bake in a preheated oven, 190°C/375°F/Gas Mark 5, for 30 minutes or until the coconut topping is firm and just golden.

7 Leave to cool in the cake tin (pan) for about 5 minutes, then cut into squares. Leave to cool completely in the tin (pan).

8 Carefully remove the squares from the tin (pan) and place them on a board. Melt the dark chocolate (if using) and drizzle it over the squares to decorate them. Leave the chocolate to set before serving.

COOK'S TIP

Store the squares in an airtight tin for up to 4 days. They can be frozen, undecorated, for up to 2 months. Defrost at room temperature.

Chocolate Orange Biscuits (Cookies)

Makes about 30

INGREDIENTS

75 g/2³/4 oz/¹/3 cup butter, softened

75 g/2³/4 oz/¹/3 cup caster (superfine) sugar

1 egg

1 tbsp milk

225 g/8 oz/2 cups plain (all-purpose) flour

25 g/1 oz/¹/4 cup cocoa powder

ICING:

175 g/6 oz/1 cup icing (confectioners') sugar, sifted

3 tbsp orange juice

a little dark chocolate, melted

1 Line 2 baking trays (cookie sheets) with sheets of baking parchment.

2 Beat together the butter and sugar until light and fluffy. Beat in the egg and milk until well combined. Sift together the flour and cocoa powder and gradually mix together to form a soft dough. Use your fingers to incorporate the last of the flour and bring the dough together.

3 Roll out the dough on to a lightly floured surface until 6 mm/¹/4 inch thick. Using a 5 cm/2 inch fluted round cutter, cut out as many cookies as you can. Re-roll the dough trimmings and cut out more cookies.

4 Place the cookies on the prepared baking tray (cookie sheet) and bake in a preheated oven, 180°C/350°F/Gas Mark 4, for 10–12 minutes or until golden.

5 Leave the cookies to cool on the baking tray (cookie sheet) for a few minutes, then transfer to a wire rack to cool completely.

6 To make the icing, place the icing (confectioners') sugar in a bowl and stir in enough orange juice to form a thin icing that will coat the back of a spoon. Spread the icing over the cookies and leave to set. Drizzle with melted chocolate. Leave the chocolate to set before serving.

Viennese Chocolate Fingers

Makes about 18

INGREDIENTS

125 g/4^1/2 oz/^{1}/2 cup unsalted
butter
75 g/2^2/3 oz/6 tbsp icing
(confectioners') sugar

175 g/6 oz/1^1/2 cups self-raising
flour, sieved (strained)
25 g/1 oz/3 tbsp cornflour
(cornstarch)

200 g/7 oz dark chocolate

1 Lightly grease 2 baking trays (cookie sheets). Beat the butter and sugar in a mixing bowl until light and fluffy. Gradually beat in the flour and cornflour (cornstarch).

2 Melt 75 g/2¾ oz of the dark chocolate and beat into the biscuit dough.

3 Place in a piping bag fitted with a large star nozzle (tip) and pipe fingers about 5 cm/2 inches long on the baking trays (cookie sheets), slightly spaced apart to allow for spreading.

4 Bake in a preheated oven, 190°C/375°F/Gas Mark 5, for 12–15 minutes. Leave to cool slightly on the baking trays (cookie sheets), then transfer with a palette knife (spatula) to a wire rack and leave to cool completely.

5 Melt the remaining chocolate and dip one end of each biscuit (cookie) in the chocolate, allowing the excess to drip back into the bowl.

6 Place the biscuits (cookies) on a sheet of baking parchment and leave to set before serving.

COOK'S TIP

If the biscuit (cookie) dough is too thick to pipe, beat in a little milk to thin it out a little.

VARIATION

Dip the base of each biscuit in melted chocolate and leave to set. Sandwich the biscuits (cookies) together in pairs with a little butter cream.

Mini Chocolate Ginger Puddings with Chocolate Custard

Serves 4

INGREDIENTS

100 g/3¹/2 oz/generous ¹/3 cup soft margarine
100 g/3¹/2 oz/³/4 cup self-raising flour, sieved (strained)
100 g/3¹/2 oz/7 tbsp caster (superfine) sugar
2 eggs
25 g/1 oz/¹/4 cup cocoa powder,

sieved (strained)
25 g/1 oz dark chocolate
50 g/1³/4 oz stem ginger

CHOCOLATE CUSTARD:
2 egg yolks
1 tbsp caster (superfine) sugar
1 tbsp cornflour (cornstarch)

300 ml/¹/2 pint/1¹/4 cups milk
100 g/3¹/2 oz dark chocolate, broken into pieces
icing (confectioners') sugar, to dust

1 Lightly grease 4 individual pudding basins. Place the margarine, flour, sugar, eggs and cocoa powder in a mixing bowl and beat until well combined and smooth. Chop the chocolate and ginger and stir into the mixture.

2 Spoon the cake mixture into the prepared basins and level the top. The mixture should three-quarters fill the basins. Cover the basins with discs of baking parchment and cover with a pleated sheet of foil. Steam for 45 minutes until the puddings are cooked and springy to the touch.

3 Meanwhile, make the custard. Beat together the egg yolks, sugar and cornflour (cornstarch) to form a smooth paste. Heat the milk until boiling and pour over the egg mixture. Return to the pan and cook over a very low heat stirring until thick. Remove from the heat and beat in the chocolate. Stir until the chocolate melts.

4 Lift the puddings from the steamer, run a knife around the edge of the basins and turn out on to serving plates. Dust with sugar and drizzle some chocolate custard over the top. Serve the remaining custard separately.

Chocolate Fudge Pudding

Serves 6

INGREDIENTS

150 g/5¹/₂ oz/generous ¹/₃ cup
    soft margarine
150 g/5¹/₂ oz/1¹/₄ cups
    self-raising flour
150 g/5¹/₂ oz/¹/₂ cup golden
    (light corn) syrup

3 eggs
25 g/1 oz/¹/₄ cup cocoa powder

CHOCOLATE FUDGE SAUCE:
100 g/3¹/₂ oz dark chocolate
125 ml/4 fl oz/¹/₂ cup sweetened
    condensed milk
4 tbsp double (heavy) cream

1 Lightly grease a 1.2 litre/2 pint/5 cup pudding basin.

2 Place the ingredients for the sponge in a mixing bowl and beat until well combined and smooth.

3 Spoon into the prepared basin and level the top. Cover with a disc of baking parchment and tie a pleated sheet of foil over the basin. Steam for 1½–2 hours until the pudding is cooked and springy to the touch.

4 To make the sauce, break the chocolate into small pieces and place in a small pan with the condensed milk. Heat gently, stirring until the chocolate melts.

5 Remove the pan from the heat and stir in the double (heavy) cream.

6 To serve the pudding, turn it out on to a serving plate and pour over a little of the chocolate fudge sauce. Serve the remaining sauce separately.

COOK'S TIP

To cook the cake in the microwave, cook it, uncovered, on High for 4 minutes, turning the basin once. Leave to stand for at least 5 minutes before turning out. Whilst the pudding is standing, make the sauce. Break the chocolate into pieces and place in a microwave-proof bowl with the milk. Cook on high for 1 minute, then stir until the chocolate melts. Stir in the double (heavy) cream and serve.

Pecan & Chocolate Fudge Ring

Serves 6

INGREDIENTS

FUDGE SAUCE:
40 g/1½ oz/3 tbsp butter
40 g/1½ oz/3 tbsp light
    muscovado sugar
4 tbsp golden (light corn) syrup
2 tbsp milk
1 tbsp cocoa powder

40 g/1½ oz dark chocolate
50 g/1¾ oz pecan nuts, finely
    chopped

CAKE:
100 g/3½ oz/generous ⅓ cup
    soft margarine

100 g/3½ oz/7 tbsp light
    muscovado sugar
125 g/4½ oz/1 cup self-raising
    flour
2 eggs
2 tbsp milk
1 tbsp golden (light corn) syrup

1 Lightly grease a
20 cm/8 inch ring
tin (pan).

2 To make the fudge
sauce, place the butter,
sugar, syrup, milk and
cocoa powder in a small
pan and heat gently, stirring
until combined.

3 Break the chocolate
into pieces, add to the
mixture and stir until
melted. Stir in the
chopped nuts. Pour into
the base of the tin (pan)
and leave to cool.

4 To make the cake,
place all of the
ingredients in a mixing
bowl and beat until
smooth. Carefully spoon
the cake mixture over the
chocolate fudge sauce.

5 Bake in a preheated
oven, 180°C/350°F/Gas
Mark 4, for 35 minutes or
until the cake is springy to
the touch.

6 Leave to cool in the tin
(pan) for 5 minutes,
then turn out on to a
serving dish and serve.

COOK'S TIP

*To make in the microwave,
place the butter, sugar, syrup,
milk and cocoa powder for
the sauce in a microwave-
proof bowl. Cook on high
for 2 minutes, stirring twice.
Stir in the chocolate until
melted, then add the nuts.
Pour into a 1.1 litre/2 pint/
5 cup microwave-proof ring
mould (mold). Make the
cake and cook on high for
3–4 minutes until just dry
on top; stand for 5 minutes.*

Chocolate Meringue Pie

Serves 6

INGREDIENTS

225 g/8 oz dark chocolate
digestive biscuits (graham
crackers)
50 g/1³/4 oz/4 tbsp butter

FILLING:
3 egg yolks

50 g/1³/4 oz/4 tbsp caster
(superfine) sugar
4 tbsp cornflour (cornstarch)
600 ml/1 pint/2¹/2 cups milk
100 g/3¹/2 oz dark chocolate,
melted

MERINGUE:
2 egg whites
100 g/3¹/2 oz/7 tbsp caster
(superfine) sugar
¹/4 tsp vanilla flavouring (extract)

1 Place the digestive biscuits (graham crackers) in a plastic bag and crush with a rolling pin. Pour into a mixing bowl. Melt the butter and stir it into the biscuit (cracker) crumbs until well mixed. Press the biscuit mixture firmly into the base and up the sides of a 23 cm/9 inch flan tin (pan) or dish.

2 To make the filling, beat the egg yolks, caster (superfine) sugar and cornflour (cornstarch) in a large bowl until they form a smooth paste, adding a little of the milk if necessary. Heat the milk until almost boiling, then slowly pour it on to the egg mixture, whisking well.

3 Return the mixture to the saucepan and cook gently, whisking constantly until it thickens. Remove from the heat. Whisk in the melted chocolate, then pour it on to the digestive biscuit (graham cracker) base.

4 To make the meringue, whisk the egg whites in a large mixing bowl until standing in soft peaks. Gradually whisk in about two-thirds of the sugar until the mixture is stiff and glossy. Fold in the remaining sugar and vanilla flavouring (extract).

5 Spread the meringue over the filling, swirling the surface with the back of a spoon to give it an attractive finish. Bake in the centre of a preheated oven, 170°C/375°F/Gas Mark 3, for 30 minutes or until the meringue is golden. Serve hot or just warm.

Chocolate & Banana Pancakes

Serves 4

INGREDIENTS

3 large bananas	2 tsp cornflour (cornstarch)	PANCAKES:
6 tbsp orange juice	3 tbsp milk	100 g/3 1/2 oz/1 cup plain
grated rind of 1 orange	40 g/1 1/2 oz dark chocolate	(all-purpose) flour
2 tbsp orange- or banana-	15 g/1/2 oz/1 tbsp butter	1 tbsp cocoa powder
flavoured liqueur	175 g/6 oz/1/2 cup golden (light	1 egg
	corn) syrup	1 tsp sunflower oil
HOT CHOCOLATE SAUCE:	1/4 tsp vanilla flavouring (extract)	300 ml/1/2 pint/1 1/4 cups milk
1 tbsp cocoa powder		oil, for frying

1 Peel and slice the bananas and arrange them in a dish with the orange juice and rind and the liqueur. Set aside.

2 Mix the cocoa powder and cornflour (cornstarch) in a bowl, then stir in the milk. Break the dark chocolate into pieces and place in a pan with the butter and golden (light corn) syrup. Heat gently, stirring until well blended. Add the cocoa mixture and bring to the boil over a gentle heat,

stirring. Simmer for 1 minute, then remove from the heat and stir in the vanilla flavouring (extract).

3 To make the pancakes, sieve (strain) the flour and cocoa into a mixing bowl and make a well in the centre. Add the egg and oil. Gradually whisk in the milk to form a smooth batter. Heat a little oil in a heavy-based frying pan (skillet) and pour off any excess. Pour in a little batter and tilt the pan to coat the base. Cook over a

medium heat until the underside is browned. Flip over and cook the other side. Slide the pancake out of the pan and keep warm. Repeat until all the batter has been used.

4 To serve, reheat the chocolate sauce for 1–2 minutes. Fill the pancakes with the bananas and fold in half or into triangles. Pour over a little chocolate sauce and serve.

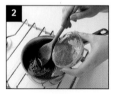

Chocolate Zabaglione

Serves 2

INGREDIENTS

4 egg yolks	50 g/1³/4 oz dark chocolate	cocoa powder, to dust
50 g/1³/4 oz/4 tbsp caster (superfine) sugar	125 ml/4 fl oz/1 cup Marsala wine	

1 In a large glass mixing bowl, whisk together the egg yolks and caster (superfine) sugar until you have a very pale mixture, using electric beaters.

2 Grate the chocolate finely and fold into the egg mixture. Fold in the wine.

3 Place the mixing bowl over a saucepan of gently simmering water and set the beaters on the lowest speed or swop to a balloon whisk. Cook gently, whisking continuously until the mixture thickens; take care not to overcook or the mixture will curdle.

4 Spoon the hot mixture into warmed individual glass dishes and dust lightly with cocoa powder. Serve the zabaglione as soon as possible so that it is warm, light and fluffy.

COOK'S TIP

For an up-to-the-minute serving idea, spoon the zabaglione into coffee cups and serve with amaretti biscuits to the side of the saucer.

COOK'S TIP

Make the dessert just before serving as the mixture will separate if left to stand. If it begins to curdle, you may be able to save it if you remove it from the heat immediately and place it in a bowl of cold water to stop the cooking. Whisk furiously until the mixture comes together.

Chocolate & Vanilla Creams

Serves 4

INGREDIENTS

450 ml/16 fl oz/2 cups double
(heavy) cream
75 g/2³/4 oz/¹/3 cup caster
(superfine) sugar
1 vanilla pod

200 ml/7 fl oz/³/4 cup crème
fraîche
2 tsp gelatine
3 tbsp water
50 g/1³/4 oz dark chocolate

MARBLED CHOCOLATE SHAPES:
a little melted white chocolate
a little melted dark chocolate

1 Place the cream and sugar in a saucepan. Cut the vanilla pod into 2 pieces and add to the cream. Heat gently, stirring until the sugar has dissolved, then bring to the boil. Reduce the heat and leave to simmer for 2–3 minutes.

2 Remove the pan from the heat and take out the vanilla pod. Stir in the crème fraîche.

3 Sprinkle the gelatine over the water in a small heatproof bowl and leave to go spongy, then place over a pan of hot water and stir until dissolved. Stir into the cream mixture. Pour half of this mixture into another mixing bowl.

4 Melt the dark chocolate and stir it into one half of the cream mixture. Pour the chocolate mixture into 4 individual glass serving dishes and chill for 15–20 minutes until just set. While it is chilling, keep the vanilla mixture at room temperature.

5 Spoon the vanilla mixture on top of the chocolate mixture and chill until the vanilla is set.

6 Meanwhile, make the shapes for the decoration. Spoon the melted white chocolate into a paper piping bag and snip off the tip. Spread some melted dark chocolate on a piece of baking parchment. Whilst still wet, pipe a fine line of white chocolate in a scribble over the top. Use the tip of a cocktail stick (toothpick) to marble the white chocolate into the dark. When firm but not too hard, cut into shapes with a small shaped cutter or a sharp knife. Chill the shapes until firm, then use to decorate the desserts.

Chocolate Hazelnut Pots

Serves 6

INGREDIENTS

2 eggs

2 egg yolks

15 g/^{1}/$_2$ oz/1 tbsp caster (superfine) sugar

1 tsp cornflour (cornstarch)

600 ml/1 pint/2^1/$_2$ cups milk

75 g/3 oz dark chocolate

4 tbsp chocolate and hazelnut spread

TO DECORATE:

grated chocolate or large chocolate curls (see page 22)

1 Beat together the eggs, egg yolks, caster (superfine) sugar and cornflour (cornstarch) until well combined. Heat the milk until almost boiling.

2 Gradually pour the milk on to the eggs, whisking as you do so. Melt the chocolate and hazelnut spread in a bowl set over a pan of gently simmering water, then whisk the melted chocolate mixture into the eggs.

3 Pour into 6 small ovenproof dishes and cover the dishes with foil.

Place them in a roasting tin (pan). Fill the tin (pan) with boiling water to come halfway up the sides of the dishes.

4 Bake in a preheated oven, 170°C/325°F/Gas Mark 3, for 35–40 minutes until the custard is just set. Remove from the tin (pan) and cool, then chill until required. Serve decorated with grated chocolate or chocolate curls.

COOK'S TIP

This dish is traditionally made in little pots called pots de crème, which are individual ovenproof dishes with a lid. Ramekins (custard pots) are fine. The dessert can also be made in one large dish; cook for about 1 hour or until set.

COOK'S TIP

The foil lid prevents a skin forming on the surface of the custards.

Layered Chocolate Mousse

Serves 8

INGREDIENTS

3 eggs
1 tsp cornflour (cornstarch)
50 g/1³/4 oz/4 tbsp caster
   (superfine) sugar
300 ml/¹/2 pint/1¹/4 cups milk

1 sachet (envelope) gelatine
3 tbsp water
300 ml/¹/2 pint/1¹/4 cups double
   (heavy) cream
75 g/2³/4 oz dark chocolate

75 g/2³/4 oz white chocolate
75 g/2³/4 oz milk chocolate
chocolate caraque, to decorate
   (see introduction)

1 Line a 450 g/1 lb loaf tin (pan) with baking parchment. Separate the eggs, putting each egg white in a separate bowl. Place the egg yolks and sugar in a large mixing bowl and whisk until well combined. Place the milk in a pan and heat gently, stirring until almost boiling. Pour the milk on to the egg yolks, whisking.

2 Set the bowl over a pan of gently simmering water and cook, stirring until the mixture thickens enough to thinly coat the back of a wooden spoon.

3 Sprinkle the gelatine over the water in a small heatproof bowl and leave to go spongy. Place over a pan of hot water and stir until dissolved. Stir into the hot mixture. Leave to cool.

4 Whip the cream until just holding its shape. Fold into the egg custard, then divide the mixture into 3. Melt the 3 types of chocolate separately. Fold the dark chocolate into one egg custard portion. Whisk one egg white until standing in soft peaks and fold into the dark chocolate custard until combined. Pour into the

prepared tin (pan) and level the top. Chill in the coldest part of the refrigerator until just set. Leave the remaining mixtures at room temperature.

5 Fold the white chocolate into another portion of the egg custard. Whisk another egg white and fold in. Pour on top of the dark chocolate layer and chill quickly. Repeat with the remaining milk chocolate and egg white. Chill until set. To serve, carefully turn out on to a serving dish and decorate with chocolate caraque.

Iced White Chocolate Terrine

Serves 8–10

INGREDIENTS

2 tbsp granulated sugar	300 g/10¹/₂ oz white chocolate	300 ml/¹/₂ pint/1¹/₄ cups double
5 tbsp water	3 eggs, separated	(heavy) cream

1 Line a 450 g/1 lb loaf tin (pan) with foil or cling film (plastic wrap), pressing out as many creases as you can.

2 Place the granulated sugar and water in a heavy-based pan and heat gently, stirring until the sugar has dissolved. Bring to the boil and boil for 1–2 minutes until syrupy, then remove the pan from the heat.

3 Break the white chocolate into small pieces and stir it into the syrup, continuing to stir until the chocolate has melted and combined with the syrup. Leave to cool slightly.

4 Beat the egg yolks into the chocolate mixture. Leave to cool completely.

5 Lightly whip the cream until just holding its shape and fold it into the chocolate mixture.

6 Whisk the egg whites in a grease-free bowl until they are standing in soft peaks. Fold into the chocolate mixture. Pour into the prepared loaf tin (pan) and freeze overnight.

7 To serve, remove from the freezer about 10–15 minutes before serving. Turn out of the tin (pan) and cut into slices to serve.

COOK'S TIP

To make a coulis, place 225 g/8 oz soft fruit of your choice – strawberries, black or red currants, mango or raspberries are ideal – in a food processor or blender. Add 1–2 tbsp icing (confectioners') sugar and blend to form a purée. If the fruit contains seeds, push the purée through a sieve to remove them. Leave to chill until required.

Baked Chocolate Alaska

Serves 6

INGREDIENTS

2 eggs
50 g/1³/4 oz/4 tbsp caster
(superfine) sugar
40 g/1¹/2 oz/generous ¹/4 cup
plain (all-purpose) flour

15 g/¹/2 oz/2 tbsp cocoa powder
3 egg whites
150 g/5¹/2 oz/²/3 cup caster
(superfine) sugar

1 litre/1³/4 pint/4¹/2 cups good
quality chocolate ice cream

1 Grease an 18 cm/7 inch round cake tin (pan) and line the base with baking parchment.

2 Whisk the egg and the 4 tbsp sugar in a mixing bowl until very thick and pale. Sieve (strain) the flour and cocoa powder together and carefully fold in.

3 Pour into the prepared tin (pan) and bake in a preheated oven, 220°C/425°F/Gas Mark 7, for 7 minutes or until springy to the touch. Transfer to a wire rack to cool completely.

4 Whisk the egg whites in a grease-free bowl until they are standing in soft peaks. Gradually add the sugar, whisking until you have a thick, glossy meringue.

5 Place the sponge on a baking tray (cookie sheet) and pile the ice cream on to the centre in a heaped dome.

6 Pipe or spread the meringue over the ice cream, making sure the ice cream is completely enclosed. (At this point the dessert can be frozen, if wished.)

7 Return it to the oven, for 5 minutes until the meringue is just golden. Serve immediately.

COOK'S TIP

This dessert is delicious served with a blackcurrant coulis. Cook a few blackcurrants in a little orange juice until soft, purée and push through a sieve, then sweeten to taste with a little icing (confectioners') sugar.

Chocolate Horns with Ginger Cardamom Cream

Serves 6

INGREDIENTS

1 egg white
50 g/1³/4 oz/4 tbsp caster (superfine) sugar
15 g/¹/2 oz/2 tbsp plain (all-purpose) flour
15 g/¹/2 oz/2 tbsp cocoa powder

25 g/1 oz/2 tbsp butter, melted
50 g/1³/4 oz dark chocolate

CARDAMOM CREAM:
150 ml/¹/4 pint/¹/3 cup double (heavy) cream

1 tbsp icing (confectioners') sugar
¹/4 tsp ground cardamom
pinch of ground ginger
25 g/1 oz stem ginger, chopped finely

1 Place a sheet of baking parchment on 2 baking trays (cookie sheets). Lightly grease 6 cream horn moulds (molds). To make the horns, beat the egg white and sugar in a mixing bowl until well combined. Sieve (strain) the flour and cocoa powder together, then beat into the egg followed by the melted butter.

2 Place 1 tablespoon of the mixture on to 1 baking tray (cookie sheet)

and spread out to form a 12.5 cm/5 inch circle. Bake in a preheated oven, 200°C/400°F/Gas Mark 6, for 4–5 minutes.

3 Working quickly, remove the biscuit (cookie) with a palette knife (spatula) and wrap around the cream horn mould (mold) to form a cone. Leave to set, then remove from the mould (mold). Repeat with the remaining mixture to make 6 cones.

4 Melt the chocolate and dip the open edges of the horn in the chocolate. Place on a piece of baking parchment and leave to set.

5 To make the cardamom cream, place the cream in a bowl and sieve (strain) the icing (confectioners') sugar and ground spices over the surface. Whisk the cream until standing in soft peaks. Fold in the chopped ginger and use to fill the chocolate cones.

Marble Cheesecake

Serves 10–12

INGREDIENTS

BASE:
225 g/8 oz toasted oat cereal
50 g/1³/4 oz/¹/2 cup toasted
   hazelnuts, chopped
50 g/1³/4 oz/4 tbsp butter
25 g/1 oz dark chocolate

FILLING:
350 g/12 oz full fat soft cheese
100 g/3¹/2 oz/7 tbsp caster
   (superfine) sugar
200 ml/7 fl oz/³/4 cup thick
   yogurt

300 ml/¹/2 pint/1¹/4 cups double
   (heavy) cream
1 sachet (envelope) gelatine
3 tbsp water
175 g/6 oz dark chocolate, melted
175 g/6 oz white chocolate,
   melted

1 Place the toasted oat cereal in a plastic bag and crush with a rolling pin. Pour the crushed cereal into a mixing bowl and stir in the hazelnuts.

2 Melt the butter and chocolate together over a low heat and stir into the cereal mixture, stirring until well coated.

3 Using the bottom of a glass, press the mixture into the base and up the sides of a 20 cm/8 inch springform tin (pan).

4 Beat together the cheese and sugar with a wooden spoon until smooth. Beat in the yogurt. Whip the cream until just holding its shape and fold into the mixture. Sprinkle the gelatine over the water in a heatproof bowl and leave to go spongy. Place over a pan of hot water and stir until dissolved. Stir into the mixture.

5 Divide the mixture in half and beat the dark chocolate into one half and the white chocolate into the other half.

6 Place alternate spoonfuls of mixture on top of the cereal base. Swirl the filling together with the tip of a knife to give a marbled effect. Level the top with a scraper or a palette knife (spatula). Leave to chill until set before serving.

COOK'S TIP

For a lighter texture, fold in 2 egg whites whipped to soft peaks before folding in the cream in step 4.

Mississippi Mud Pie

Serves 8–10

INGREDIENTS

225 g/8 oz/2 cups plain (all-purpose) flour
25 g/1 oz/¼ cup cocoa powder
150 g/5½ oz/⅔ cup butter
25 g/1 oz/5 tsp caster (superfine) sugar
about 2 tbsp cold water

FILLING:
175 g/6 oz/¾ cup butter
350 g/12 oz dark muscovado sugar
4 eggs, lightly beaten
4 tbsp cocoa powder, sieved (strained)
150 g/5½ oz dark chocolate

300ml/½ pt single (light) cream
1 tsp chocolate flavouring (extract)

TO DECORATE:
425 ml/¾ pint/1¾ cups double (heavy) cream, whipped
thick bar of chocolate

1 To make the pastry (pie dough), sieve (strain) the flour and cocoa powder into a mixing bowl. Rub in the butter until the mixture resembles fine breadcrumbs. Stir in the sugar and enough cold water to mix to a soft dough. Chill for 15 minutes.

2 Roll out the dough on a lightly floured surface and use to line a deep 23 cm/ 9 inch loose-bottomed flan tin (pan) or ceramic flan dish. Line with foil or baking parchment and baking beans. Bake blind in a preheated oven, 190°C/375°F/Gas Mark 5, for 15 minutes. Remove the beans and foil or paper and cook for a further 10 minutes until crisp.

3 To make the filling, beat the butter and sugar in a bowl and gradually beat in the eggs with the cocoa powder. Melt the chocolate and beat it into the mixture with the single (light) cream and the chocolate flavouring (extract).

4 Pour the mixture into the cooked pastry case and bake at 170°C/ 325°F/Gas Mark 3 for 45 minutes or until the filling is set.

5 Leave to cool completely, then transfer the pie to a serving plate, if preferred. Cover with the whipped cream and leave to chill.

6 To make small chocolate curls, use a potato peeler to remove curls from the bar of chocolate. Decorate the pie and leave to chill.

No-Cook Fruit & Nut Chocolate Fudge

Makes about 25 pieces

INGREDIENTS

250 g/9 oz dark chocolate
25 g/1 oz/2 tbsp butter
4 tbsp evaporated milk
450 g/1 lb/3 cups icing

(confectioners') sugar, sieved
(strained)
50 g/1³/4 oz/¹/2 cup roughly
chopped hazelnuts

50 g/1³/4 oz/¹/3 cup sultanas
(golden raisins)

1 Lightly grease a
20 cm/8 inch square
cake tin (pan).

2 Break the chocolate
into pieces and place it
in a bowl with the butter
and evaporated milk. Set
the bowl over a pan of
gently simmering water and
stir until the chocolate and
butter have melted and the
ingredients are well
combined.

3 Remove the bowl
from the heat and
gradually beat in the icing
(confectioners') sugar. Stir

the hazelnuts and sultanas
(golden raisins) into the
mixture. Press the fudge into
the prepared tin (pan) and
level the top. Chill until firm.

4 Tip the fudge out on to
a chopping board and
cut into squares. Place in
paper sweet (candy) cases.
Chill until required.

VARIATION

*Vary the nuts used in this
recipe; try making the fudge
with almonds, brazil nuts,
walnuts or pecans.*

COOK'S TIP

*The fudge can be stored in
an airtight container for up
to 2 weeks.*

Chocolate Cups with Mascarpone Filling

Makes 20

INGREDIENTS

100 g/3 1/2 oz dark chocolate

FILLING:
100 g/3 1/2 oz milk or dark
chocolate
1/4 tsp vanilla flavouring (extract)

200 g/7 oz mascarpone cheese
cocoa powder, to dust

1 Line a baking tray (cookie sheet) with a sheet of baking parchment. Melt the chocolate and spoon it into 20 paper sweet (candy) cases, spreading up the sides with a small spoon or pastry brush. Place upside down on the prepared baking tray (cookie sheet) and leave to set.

2 When set, carefully peel away the paper cases.

3 To make the filling, melt the dark or milk chocolate. Place the mascarpone cheese in a bowl and beat in the vanilla flavouring (extract) and melted chocolate and beat until well combined. Leave the mixture to chill, beating occasionally until firm enough to pipe.

4 Place the mascarpone filling in a piping bag fitted with a star nozzle (tip) and pipe the mixture into the cups. Decorate with a dusting of cocoa powder.

COOK'S TIP

Mascarpone is a rich Italian soft cheese made from fresh cream, so it has a high fat content. Its delicate flavour blends well with chocolate.

VARIATION

You can use lightly whipped double (heavy) cream instead of the mascarpone cheese, if preferred.

Champagne Mousse

Serves 4

INGREDIENTS

SPONGE:
4 eggs
100 g/3¹/2 oz/7 tbsp caster
    (superfine) sugar
75 g/2³/4 oz/²/3 cup self-raising
    flour
15 g/¹/4 oz/2 tbsp cocoa powder
25 g/1 oz/2 tbsp butter, melted

MOUSSE:
1 sachet (envelope) gelatine
3 tbsp water
300 ml/¹/2 pint/1¹/4 cups
    champagne
300 ml/¹/2 pint/1¹/4 cups double
    (heavy) cream
2 egg whites

75 g/2³/4 oz/¹/3 cup caster
    (superfine) sugar

TO DECORATE:
50 g/2 oz dark chocolate-
    flavoured cake covering,
    melted
fresh strawberries

1 Line a 37.5 x 25 cm/15 x 10 inch Swiss roll tin (pan) with greased baking parchment. Place the eggs and sugar in a bowl and whisk with electric beaters until the mixture is very thick and the whisk leaves a trail when lifted. If using a balloon whisk, stand the bowl over a pan of hot water whilst whisking. Sieve (strain) the flour and cocoa together and fold into the egg mixture. Fold in the butter. Pour into the tin (pan) and bake in a preheated oven, 200°C/ 400°F/Gas Mark 6, for 8 minutes or until springy to the touch. Cool for 5 minutes, then turn out on to a wire rack until cold. Line four 10 cm/4 inch baking rings with baking parchment. Line the sides with 2.5 cm/1 inch strips of cake and the base with circles.

2 To make the mousse, sprinkle the gelatine over the water and leave to go spongy. Place the bowl over a pan of hot water; stir until dissolved. Stir in the champagne.

3 Whip the cream until just holding its shape. Fold in the champagne mixture. Leave in a cool place until on the point of setting, stirring. Whisk the egg whites until standing in soft peaks, add the sugar and whisk until glossy. Fold into the setting mixture. Spoon into the sponge cases, allowing the mixture to go above the sponge. Chill for 2 hours. Pipe the cake covering in squiggles on a piece of parchment; leave to set. Decorate the mousses.

Hot Chocolate Drinks

Serves 2

INGREDIENTS

SPICY HOT CHOCOLATE:
600 ml/1 pint/2^1/2 cups milk
1 tsp ground mixed spice
    (allspice)
100 g/3^1/2 oz dark chocolate
4 cinnamon sticks

100 ml/3^1/2 fl oz/^{1}/3 cup double
(heavy) cream, lightly
whipped

HOT CHOCOLATE & ORANGE
TODDY:
75 g/2^1/2 oz orange-flavoured
    dark chocolate

600 ml/1 pint/2^1/2 cups milk
3 tbsp rum
2 tbsp double (heavy) cream
grated nutmeg

1 To make Spicy Hot
Chocolate, pour the
milk into a small pan.
Sprinkle in the mixed spice
(allspice).

2 Break the dark
chocolate into squares
and add to the milk. Heat
the mixture over a low
heat until the milk is just
boiling, stirring all the
time to prevent the milk
burning on the bottom of
the pan.

3 Place 2 cinnamon sticks
in 2 cups and pour in

the spicy hot chocolate. Top
with the whipped double
(heavy) cream and serve.

4 To make Hot
Chocolate &
Orange Toddy, break the
orange-flavoured dark
chocolate into squares
and place in a small
saucepan with the milk.
Heat over a low heat until
just boiling, stirring
constantly.

5 Remove the pan from
the heat and stir in the
rum. Pour into cups.

6 Pour the cream over the
back of a spoon or swirl
on to the top so that it sits on
top of the hot chocolate.
Sprinkle with grated nutmeg
and serve at once.

COOK'S TIP

*Using a cinnamon stick as a
stirrer will give any hot
chocolate drink a sweet,
pungent flavour of cinnamon
without overpowering the
flavour of the chocolate.*

This is a Parragon Book
First published in 2000

Parragon
Queen Street House
4 Queen Street
Bath BA1 1HE, UK

ISBN: 0-75253-617-6

Printed in China

Note

Cup measurements in this book are for American cups. Tablespoons are assumed to be
15 ml. Unless otherwise stated, milk is assumed to be full fat, eggs are medium and
pepper is freshly ground black pepper.